SUSSEX
A Visitor's Sketchbook

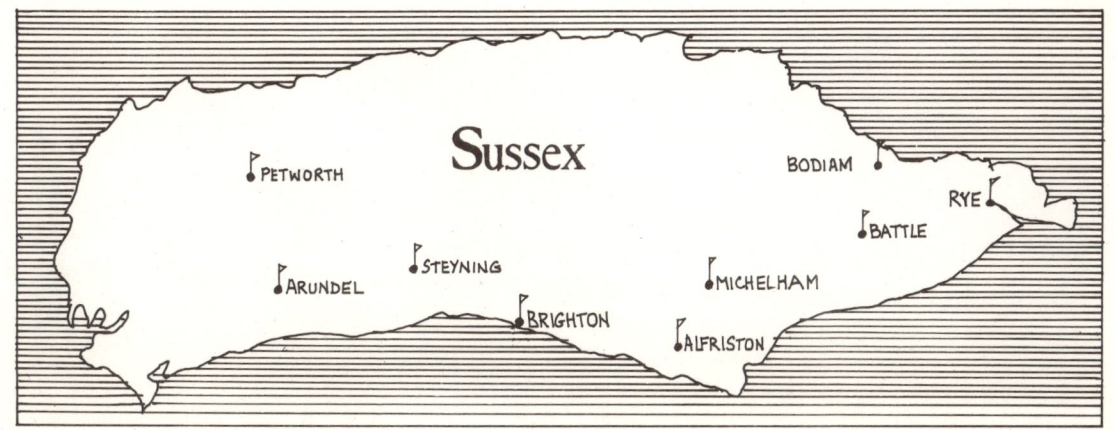

Sussex

PETWORTH

BODIAM

RYE

BATTLE

STEYNING

ARUNDEL

MICHELHAM

BRIGHTON

ALFRISTON

SUSSEX
A Visitor's Sketchbook

Illustrations by
DAVID ARMITAGE
Text by PENNY VISMAN

Pekoe Books

To all the societies and countless good people who have tirelessly worked to preserve the county heritage.

First published in Great Britain in 1987 by
Pekoe Books Ltd, The Manor,
Whitestaunton, Chard, Somerset

Britith Library Cataloguing in Publication Data

Armitage, David, 1943—
    Sussex: a visitor's sketchbook.—
    (A Pekoe pictorial).
    1. Sussex — Description and travel —
    Views
    I. Title   II. Visman, Penny
    914.22'504858'0222   DA670.S98

ISBN 1–870537–00–9

Designed by David Armitage

Phototypeset in Palatino by Falcon Graphic Art Ltd
Wallington, Surrey

Colour reproduction by
South Sea International Press Ltd, London

Monochrome reproduction by
Prostats Ltd, Tonbridge, Kent

Contents

A tribute to Sussex

SUSSEX is traditionally a 'singular' county. Historians have written in depth about the reasons for the insularity and quiet obstinacy of the inhabitants, which inhibited even the one-time Roman occupiers: their roads, in other parts built in dead straight lines, were in this county given curious twists and turns. Much is recorded of the character of Sussex folk, for instance, their view of 'furriners' (a term which apparently applied even to those in adjoining counties), and of the way in which Sussex became a 'kingdom' in its own right, complete with dialect, itself the subject of learned works. It was not an accident that Stella Gibbons's parody of rural life, *Cold Comfort Farm* was set in the shadow of the Sussex Downs.

It is the purpose of this sketchbook to bring to life, by means of original pictures and specially written text, some of the outstanding features of the county. The aim of this introduction is to put these features into perspective.

There is a general welcoming air about Sussex but evidence of the historic roots is always near the surface. *Sussex by the Sea* is played and sung with the fervour usually accorded a national anthem. The county motto remains intact: 'We Wun't be Druv'.

Legends abound, and there is an air of the mystique. The Sussex Downs, at times brooding, but always magnificent, have defied efforts of painters to capture their true colours, and the secret of the dewponds, high up in the chalk, has never been found: attempts at their reconstruction have ever failed. Men of substance have testified to meeting ghosts in ancient Mayfield (the domain of the renowned St Dunstan), and elsewhere; to circle Chanctonbury Ring after midnight is to tempt fate; the Long Man, near the Saxon village of Wilmington, outlined in white and the tallest chalk figure in England, is of inexplicable origin. Remains of dinosaurs, the greatest being some twenty-four feet in length, have been found. Other fossils have seemed to confirm the many dragon legends, as do the mysterious pools including the Lyminster one where the water 'never freezes'.

The Lyminster dragon is reputed to have been sighted as late as the seventeenth century and is described in writings of that time. A famous dragon-slayer was St Leonard, in whose memory St Leonard's Forest, near Horsham is named. Also near here is Dragon's Green.

Sussex is rich in period churches, from the two oldest in the county, at

Fletching and at Sompting, to the cathedrals at Chichester and Arundel. Quaint villages are to be found, sometimes off the beaten track, such as Clayton at the foot of the Downs below the twin windmills, Jack and Jill, Kingston, near Lewes, East Chiltington; and towns and villages where the very spirit of bygone days lives on: Steyning, seemingly unchanged since the stage-coach; Midhurst, with its Knockhundred Row; Petworth, attached to the walls of the great estate; Billingshurst, once a staging post; and Lewes. Lewes, with its green on which bowls have been played since the sixteenth century, the Barbican and castle, is built on Downland, as evidenced by the numerous steep hills and alleys, and is truly an 'historic County Town'.

The long coastline holds a continuous string of towns and villages, stretching from Rye through Hastings (formerly the South Saxon Folk Settlement of Hæstingas) to the Witterings in the West.

Inland is much of interest: old Burwash, with Rudyard Kipling's house, Bateman's; and the villages of Ashdown Forest and the Weald. Although Saxon and Roman influence is widespread perhaps the Roman connection is more evident in the west of the county, which contains the largest Roman villa of Bignor with twelve mosaic floors, and the attractive twin County Town of Chichester.

Among good vantage points are Devil's Dyke with its views in all directions, Ditchling Beacon, high above the old village, and Cissbury Ring where, on a clear day, one may see the Isle of Wight across the water (the Palace pier at Brighton can claim an equal view) and the Seven Sisters of Seaford to the East.

It is worthy of comment that iron was found in Sussex in Roman times, and was smelted with charcoal for the manufacture of cannon and other ironware. The names 'Huggett's Furnace' and 'Huggett's Farm' near Hadlow Down are reminders of the ironmaster 'Master Huggett' and 'his man John'. A parallel discovery of coal might well have changed the face of Sussex as it is today.

SUSSEXIAN

The keep of Lewes Castle set on a mound high above the town

8

Arundel Castle

THE solid, sombre outline of Arundel Castle dominates the hillside above the small, steep Sussex town from which it takes its name. The original castle, with wooden fortifications, was built by the First Earl of Arundel, Roger de Montomery, who was rewarded by William the Conqueror with the magnificent gift of one third of the county of Sussex, as thanks for his presence in Normandy during the Battle of Hastings.

Arundel Castle has had numerous additions, restorations and rebuildings over the centuries, and several early changes of ownership. Since 1556 the castle has been the property of the Dukes of Norfolk, Earl Marshalls of England.

During the Civil War the castle was beseiged and attacked by Parliamentary forces, and it lay in ruins until the eighteenth century. The first reconstruction was started by the eleventh Duke, Charles, a friend of the Prince Regent, and a keen amateur architect. The main restoration was carried out by the fifteenth Duke, Henry, who also played a leading role in Catholic affairs in the late nineteenth century. The whole castle was restored and reconstructed between 1875 and 1900.

Arundel Castle is now vested in a special charitable trust to ensure its permanent preservation.

The entrance to the castle is over a wooden drawbridge, and through the Barbican which dates from 1295. The marks made by cannon balls fired by the Parliamentary forces in the seige of the castle in 1643 can still be seen on the walls above the archway. The eleventh-century inner gateway is one of the earliest parts of the castle still in existence. The Keep was built in 1138 with Caen stone, and now has a walled walkway from which there are extensive views of the sea, the town and the Cathedral. A banner is always flown from the well-tower of the Keep when the Duke of Norfolk is in residence.

The interior rooms, painstakingly reconstructed by Victorian craftsmen, provide the setting for some fine examples of French, German, Italian furniture and paintings.

The private chapel, built by the fifteenth Duke in the Early English Gothic style, at the end of the nineteenth century, has Purbeck marble columns supporting a stone vaulted ceiling. Ecclesiastical art treasures include a

Flemish triptych of 'The Adoration of the Magi', a rococo triptych of carved
rosewood, ivory, tortoiseshell and mother-of-pearl, and a Flemish painting of
'Christ in the Garden of Gethsemane'.

The picture gallery is lined with portraits of the Dukes and Duchesses of
Norfolk, giving a chronological pictorial history of the owners and
inhabitants of the castle. Two of the most interesting seem to have been 'The
Collector Earl', and 'The Poet Earl'.

The dining room, which was originally a chapel, has the portrait of the
twelfth Duke in parliamentary robes, which was painted to celebrate the
passing of the Catholic Emancipation Act in 1829. The robes illustrated in the
painting are those still worn by the present Duke for the State Opening of
Parliament each year. The dining room also has a set of mid-eighteenth-
century chairs with needlepoint covers, and four painted satinwood
cupboards which contain trays for hot charcoal and racks for warming plates.
Gold cups, presented at their Coronation by Sovereigns since King George II
to the Earl Marshalls of England are on display amongst other treasures.

There are portraits of children below a Gobelin tapestry on the great
staircase, and portraits by Van Dyck, Gainsborough and Reynolds in the
drawing room. A famous portrait of Cardinal Newman by Sir John Millais
hangs in the bedroom which was prepared for a visit of Queen Victoria in
1846. The library has some 10,000 books, and a collection of manuscripts
relating to Catholic history. Built of carved Honduras mahogany,
incorporating slender columns and ceiling vaulting, the library was built by
the eleventh Duke in 1800. The Chinese lanterns echo the contemporary
vogue for the oriental style. The serene silver icon was made by Fabergé for
the fifteenth Duke in 1908.

In the east drawing room there is a permanent collection of robes and
costumes, including the Earl Marshall's state uniform, Peer's Coronation
robes, and Mantles of the Orders of the Garter, Bath and Thistle. Also on
display are the illuminated prayer book and gold rosary carried by Mary,
Queen of Scots, to her execution, and bequeathed by her to the family.

Another view of Arundel Castle

The Fitzalan Chapel

The Fitzalan-Howards, the family name of the Dukes of Norfolk, are a Roman Catholic family, and they have a private Roman Catholic chapel which forms the east end of the Anglican parish church of St Nicholas in Arundel. The chapel is only accessible from the castle precincts, as a glass screen separates it from the main body of the church. This chapel was built in 1380, desecrated in 1643, and restored to the fifteenth Duke in 1886. Some original fragments have been incorporated in the rebuilding. The chapel contains the tombs and monuments of the Earls of Arundel and Dukes of Norfolk, dating from the fifteenth to the twentieth centuries.

Right. The Fitzalan Chapel

14

The City Cross, Chichester, was given to the town by Bishop Story in 1501

The spire of Chichester Cathedral soars
277 feet above the rooftops of the city

Battle Abbey

THE date 1066 still holds a *frisson* of excitement for British people. The one date that every schoolchild remembers, and the last time there was a successful invasion of Britain. The Benedictine Abbey of St. Martin, in the East Sussex town of Battle, generally known as Battle Abbey, was built by William the Conqueror, not only to commemorate his victory at the Battle of Hastings, but also to honour the dead of the battle and atone for bloodshed.

William the Conqueror insisted that the abbey be built on the scene of the fiercest fighting, and the high altar of the church be placed where Harold fell. This choice of site on high sloping ground caused much difficulty in building, as can be seen in the cross-section of construction visible in the ruins at the southern end of the east range. Norman monks were brought from the Benedictine Abbey of Marmoutier on the Loire to set up a community and supervise the building, and the abbey was consecrated in 1076.

By the fourteenth century Battle Abbey was greatly involved in the defence of the south-east coast against the continuing French raids, fulfilling another of William the Conqueror's aims—that it guard a part of the country which he himself had proved to be a good invasion route.

The Great Gatehouse, which still dominates the town, was rebuilt in 1338 as a fortification and stronghold, the design incorporating arrow slits, portcullis and crenellated parapets.

The abbey was demolished in 1538, during the Dissolution of the Monasteries as commanded by King Henry VIII, so that apart from the gatehouse and the west range of the abbey cloister, the buildings are in ruins.

Visitors can follow the indicated 'Field of Hastings' walk, which follows the terrace along the ridge overlooking the battlefield. Inside the remains of the guesthouse there is a fascinating model of the battle, with a proportion of the 14,000 Saxon and Norman soldiers in battledress, facing each other before the start of the Battle of Hastings. This guesthouse was built as a possible lodging for Princess Elizabeth, later Elizabeth the First, after the abbey had been destroyed. The thirteenth-century vaulted undercrofts were probably used as storerooms for the monastic guesthouses.

The abbey church is completely in ruins, but nineteenth-century excavations have revealed the crypt chapels and an outline plan of the church can be seen. Built in the style of contemporary churches in Normandy, this church is thought to be the first in England to combine a semicircular aisle inside the east end of the church behind the altar (ambulatory). The cloister to the south of the church was built in a traditional Benedictine layout, and the cloister walk is indicated by gravel paths. One of the best preserved and most atmospheric ruins is the novices' chamber at the south end of the eastern range, with marble columns, deep vaulting, and remains of a fireplace with tiled fireback.

A plan of the abbey shows the position and use of all the buildings now in ruins, and also the dates of building and additions from the eleventh century to the sixteenth century.

A signpost at the west end of the terrace indicates a country walk around the battlefield, and even though in ruins, Battle Abbey set in the heart of what is now called '1066 Country' is one of the most stirring and emotive sites in Britain.

Herstmonceux - one of the most splendid English houses of the 15th century

18

Bodiam Castle

BODIAM Castle, rising out of the quiet Sussex countryside, seems to be the very embodiment of castles from story-books. Massive pale walls, topped by both round and square towers, are mirrored in a wide, deep moat, the whole guarded by a great gatehouse, complete with portcullis. The charming simplicity of the design, combined with the solid show of strength, have great visual and emotive appeal, and so it comes as no surprise to learn that the castle may be closed for brief periods on one or two days for television filming.

The castle was built by Sir Edward Dalyngrigge, during 1385–8, for the defence of the Rother Valley from the raids of the French, which were then taking place on the south coast of England. In those days the River Rother was navigable up to Bodiam and regarded as part of the old port of Winchelsea. A royal licence was issued to Sir Edward by King Richard II 'to strengthen and crenellate his manor house of Bodyham near the sea in the County of Sussex with a wall of stone and lime, and to construct and make thereof a castle in defence of the adjacent countryside and for resistance against our enemies.' However, instead of fortifying his own house, Sir Edward built Bodiam Castle as a fortress near the river, from where an attack could be expected. Before completion of the castle, England regained control of the Channel in 1387, and Bodiam was never put to the test for which it was built.

During the years before he returned to Bodiam to build this fortress, Sir Edward Dalyngrigge had served in the French Wars under Sir Robert Knollys, and historians have noted that the plan of Bodiam Castle bears a certain resemblance to the much larger Chateau du Villaudrant near Bordeaux, where Sir Edward attended the court of Edward, the Black Prince. The coat of arms of Sir Robert Knollys is depicted on the tower of the Gate House, as is that of Sir Edward Dalyngrigge, with its fascinating unicorn head.

Bodiam was one of the last castle fortresses to be built before the development of the use of gunpowder and cannons made such buildings obsolete. In the Gate House, among the vaulted ribs which remain, pierced bosses can be seen, from which boiling oil or quicklime could be poured down onto invaders. The arched openings under the parapet of the Postern Gate could also be used for this purpose.

Although the interior of the castle is in ruins, a ground plan displayed near the entrance gives details of the location, size and uses of the rooms. There are thirty-three fireplaces still visible, and ten stone spiral staircases. The Chapel is easily recognised with its pointed window lights which have been partly restored. The kitchen has two huge fireplaces, both twelve feet wide, and an oven. There is still water in the ten-foot-deep well, and the pigeon loft, which was a basic source of food for castle life, has almost 200 nesting boxes still in evidence.

In 1483, almost a hundred years after it was built, the then Lancastrian owner of Bodiam surrendered to the Yorkists in the Wars of the Roses. During the Civil War the interior of Bodiam was dismantled by the Parliamentary Forces in 1644. For the next two centuries Bodiam belonged to various landowning local families who prevented its demolition. In 1916 the castle was purchased by Marques Curzon of Kedleston, who carried out extensive repairs and excavations to arrest further decay, and on his death in 1925 he bequeathed Bodiam to the care of The National Trust.

In the north-east corner of the ground between the castle and the car park, there is a brick and concrete strong point, which was erected in 1940, as part of a line of defence against German invasion, which, fortunately, like the castle, was not put to the test.

Bayham Abbey, the most complete of Sussex monastic sites

Mermaid Street, Rye

ERMAID street, in the heart of Rye, with its eclectic mix of well-preserved old houses, is one of the most unspoilt and visually appealing thoroughfares in England. White-painted weatherboard cottages, elegant Georgian town houses and mellow half-timbered Tudor buildings line the steep 'kidney' cobbled street which encompasses a fascinating slice of British history.

The pastel colours of many of the pretty houses lend a Continental atmosphere, as do the carefully nurtured climbing plants which cling to walls in tiny garden terraces, and the flower-filled pots and hanging baskets which enhance Georgian doors and fanlights. Brass lanterns, knobs and knockers, some fashioned in the form of fish or anchors, evoke maritime connections, and several houses still sport decorative Fire Marks, which were original proof of fire insurance cover. Most of the houses have locally made ceramic name-plates which provide a charming glimpse of local history and laconic humour. Names such as *First House, House with the Seat, House with the Two Front Doors, Robin Hill, Samuel Jeakes House 1689, Harthshorn House, The Old Hospital 15th Century, Quakers House, Elders House,* and *Gull, Neptune* and *Mermaid Cottages,* as well as *Moonrakers,* must all have their own story. While *The House Opposite* (opposite the Mermaid Inn) speaks for itself, and *The Owner's House,* adjoining the Inn, offers a micro history on its door plate, inscribed:

> Around 1760/1775 in common with many timbered properties, the fashion was to implant brickwork on the frontage — the four Georgian-type sash windows were probably put in a little earlier. The two top dormer windows remained in leaded lights. Viewed from Mermaid Street you will see on the ground floor the extra thickness of brickwork extending out and also a bricked-up entrance which led to the main kitchen area and was probably a Tradesman's entrance serving the whole of the oldest front area of the inn. Most of the cellars seem to have always been used for the Inn's food storage.

The Mermaid Inn itself, which proudly bears the plate 'Rebuilt in 1420', was once as much a haven for local smugglers as it is now an idyllic retreat for visitors who like to travel back in time, and much of the history of Mermaid Street, as indeed that of the town of Rye itself is distilled in the history of the Mermaid Inn.

In 1156, the then prosperous *harbour* of Rye was admitted to the membership of the Cinque Ports, and the barrel-vaulted wine cellars of the Mermaid Inn date from this time. The original inn, along with all the other timber buildings of Rye, was destroyed in the French raids of 1377/78, and the present inn was rebuilt on the same site in 1420.

The proximity to France has always been a key issue in the fortunes of Rye. In 1530, during the Reformation, the Mermaid Inn sheltered Catholic priests fleeing to the Continent, and the then forbidden letters J.H.S. (Jesus Homnium Salvator) can be seen carved in the oak panelling in what is now called 'Dr. Syn's Lounge'. There is a priest-hole visible inside the great fireplace in the lounge bar, and a secret staircase hidden behind a bookcase in 'Dr Syn's Bedchamber'.

In 1573, Queen Elizabeth the First visited Rye, and dubbed the town 'Rye Royal'. Documents show that the Mermaid Inn was used for formal occasions and celebrations, such as Sessions Dinners and Mayoring Days, during the 200 years 1550–1750, and the bills detail the sumptious feasts which were prepared. During these years Rye was the main cross-Channel port, and the Rye—Boulogne sailing packet ran a regular service, which connected to London by stage-coach. But it is the smuggling activities associated with Rye and the Mermaid Inn which now hold the most fascination. Due to restrictions on the export of wool, for economic and political reasons, much illegal trading was carried out by smugglers, who exchanged wool for brandy, wine, tobacco and lace. The notorious Hawkhurst gang of smugglers, which at times numbered several hundred men, used the Mermaid Inn as their headquarters throughout the late seventeenth and most of the eighteenth centuries. A local report records 'A gentleman born in Rye in 1740 remembered when the Hawkhurst Gang of smugglers were at the height of their pride and insolence, having seen them (after successfully having run a cargo of goods on the seashore) seated at the window of the Mermaid Inn, carousing and smoking their pipes with their loaded pistols lying on the table before them, no magistrate daring to interfere with them'. In 1737 the Bailiff of Sussex was dragged from the Mermaid Inn by a smuggler released on bail, and rescued from a boat in the harbour by the Revenue sloop. Reforms in the Customs Service eventually abolished smuggling by the mid-nineteenth century.

The Clock of St Mary the Virgin, Rye

The turret clock of St. Mary's Church is one of the famous sights of Rye. Made in 1560, the clock has 'quarter boys' which strike the quarter- and half-hours — gilded cherub-like figures on either side of the clock face. The clock tower is open to visitors and by climbing up the steep stairs in the twisting narrow passage it is possible to see the maze of wheels, cogs and levers which make up the workings of the clock. Bell ringers will be fascinated by the details in the clock tower of 'Plain Bob Triples' and 'Grandsire Doubles'.

Michelham Priory

SURROUNDED by a wide deep moat, the mellow stone buildings of Michelham Priory, set amongst sweeping lawns and ancient trees, emanate utter peace and tranquility. Built within the bend of the Cuckmere River, this historic group of buildings, which includes a fourteenth century gatehouse, Tudor great barn, and working water mill, seem to be the very essence of an Arcadian English scene.

Michelham Priory was founded in 1229, for the Augustinian Order, by the Norman Lord of Pevensey, Gilbert de 'Aigle, and in 1979, to celebrate the 750 years since the founding of the priory, the coat of arms of Gilbert of the Eagle was adopted as the house-flag of the property, and is now flown from the gatehouse.

During the Dissolution of the Monasteries, Michelham Priory was the first monastic property to be given to Thomas Cromwell, and the buildings were destroyed in 1536. After recent excavations a ground plan of the original monastic lay-out has been drawn up, which shows the position of the church, cloisters, chapter house and dormitory. Remaining fragments of the refectory have been incorporated in the building which took place towards the end of the sixteenth century when the estate became a working farm. Generations of tenant farmers were employed by several changes of owners over the centuries, until 1959, when the buildings and grounds were presented to the Sussex Archaeological Society, for preservation and public enjoyment. During the Second World War, Canadian forces lived in Michelham Priory, and an interesting map of the English Channel, drawn by them as part of a training programme for the raid on Dieppe in 1942, can be seen in the upper room of the gatehouse.

Entrance to the interior is through a vaulted room, believed to be unique in England in that the ribs of the vaulting meet in groups of three, to represent the Holy Trinity, rather than the usual groups of four. The Tudor kitchen has a large open hearth, and the chimney has two shafts — one for smoking meats and the other with a spit-driven mechanism. Period furniture, which was donated with the house, and other exhibits, are displayed and listed in each room. From April to September each year, when the priory is open to the public, there are changing art exhibitions, musical recitals, craft exhibitions, morris dancing, and many other varied events held in the priory buildings.

Monasteries were often founded near to rivers, to ensure water supplies, and many had their own mills for grinding corn. The first recorded water mill at Michelham Priory was built in 1434, and the present mill has been rebuilt several times, reusing some original material. The main timber framing is of fifteenth-century oak, and part of the early stonework is still in existence, eighteenth-century brickwork and nineteenth-century weatherborarding have also been incorporated. The only original piece of machinery that remains is the sack hoist which is on the top floor of the mill. A new water wheel and machinery has been installed, and the mill now produces stone ground wholemeal flour which is for sale — a leaflet giving traditional recipes for using this flour is available.

The latest addition to Michelham, which is both interesting and charming, is the Physic Garden, laid in 1981. Groups of herbs used as remedies by the monks who practised medicine or 'physic' are planted in sections according to the parts of the body they were believed to heal — herbs for wounds and broken bones, herbs for bites, stings, burns and poisons, herbs for depression, insomnia and nightmares, — are grown, as well as the more well-known herbs for the household.

The idyllic island site of Michelham Priory can best be appreciated from the Moat Walk, which affords varying views of the buildings and grounds, as well as glimpses of abundant wildlife.

Bateman's (Burwash), the house where Rudyard Kipling spent the last three decades of his life

Petworth House

THE first Petworth House was built in 1309, as a Manor House for the Percy family, Dukes of Northumberland, whose ancestors came over with William the Conqueror, and were subsequently rewarded with land in several counties. The present house was rebuilt in the late seventeenth century by the sixth Duke of Somerset, to whom it had passed by marriage. The only remains of the original house are the fourteenth-century chapel, and the cellars, which have been incorporated in the rebuilding.

Cognoscenti of fine art visit Petworth for the astonishingly rich collection of paintings, sculpture, porcelain and antique furniture which are so well displayed in the elegant rooms — particularly on the 'Connoisseurs' Days' when extra rooms are opened.

All the main rooms are virtual art galleries, each with its own catalogue of paintings, where such artists as Van Dyke, Holbein, Hobbema, Titian, Gainsborough, Reynolds, Lely, Bosch, and most of all the English artist J.M.W. Turner are represented.

Record and receipt books kept at Petworth over the centuries have documented many details about the costs of artistic work, and fees paid to artists and craftsmen. The first recorded item of sculpture is the copy of Michelangelo's *Pietà*, now standing in a niche which marks the position of the medieval west window of the chapel, bought by the sixth Duke of Somerset for £108 in 1691.

The collection of antique sculptures and some of the Old Masters were bought in Rome, by the second Earl of Egremont whilst on a Grand Tour, to whom the house passed in 1750. However, the main collection of outstanding paintings was acquired by the 3rd Earl of Egremont, patron of Turner and other contemporary artists, who also built the North Gallery to display his treasures.

Turner became a great friend of his patron, and a regular visitor to Petworth House, where he was given his own studio above the chapel; his sketchbook of watercolours of the interiors is now in the British Museum. The Turner Room at Petworth has a collection of his paintings including views of Petworth Lake, various scenes on the Thames, and other typically English landscapes. Other works by Turner are in the North Gallery, as well as some by Reynolds, Gainsborough and other eighteenth- and nineteenth-century artists.

The Carved Room has many exquisite examples of the work of another legendary Englishman, Grinling Gibbons, who fashioned cupids, musical instruments, birds, and baskets of fruit and flowers from wood with extraordinary skill and finesse. The Duke of Somerset's receipt book for December 1692 has an entry 'a Bill paid to Mr. Gibbons for carveing £150'.

Each of the rooms has a 'theme' — for example the Somerset Room has a collection of 17th century Dutch School paintings; the Beauty Room has a series of portraits of the ladies of the Court of Queen Anne; and the Chapel Corridor has works by William Blake depicting scenes from *Paradise Lost*, *The Last Judgement* and *Characters from Spenser's 'Faerie Queene'*.

The fine antique furniture, beautifully arranged, is from various periods, and details are listed room by room. The pieces include some items imported from Italy and Japan, as well as some good examples of English furniture in the chinoiserie style.

Superb porcelain is also itemised, and examples of Chelsea 'Red Anchor', Sèvres, Meissen, Chinese k'ang-hsi period (1622–1722), Chinese Chien-Lung period (1736–95) and Japanese Kakiemon are on display.

The charming Deer Park and delightful gardens of Petworth House were landscaped by the famous 'Capability' Brown in 1752 — and records show that many of the ancient trees still in existence — huge limes, planes and sweet chestnut trees — were planted by him.

Chanctonbury Ring – a prehistoric circular earthwork. The trees were planted in 1760

The Royal Pavilion, Brighton

THE Royal Pavilion is one of the most exotic and fascinating royal palaces in Europe. Oriental-style architecture, incorporating onion domes and minarets, creates a surprising dream-like quality, in contrast to the very English setting of Brighton. The interior of the Pavilion, with its outstanding collection of chinoiserie, is a superb memorial to the 'Chinese Taste' so beloved of connoisseurs from the seventeenth century onwards, which reached its zenith in the Regency period.

Most of all, the fabulous Pavilion is a monument to King George IV of England, who, in his dazzling days as Prince Regent, was known as 'The First Gentleman of Europe'. At the age of twenty-one the prince made his first visit to Brighton, and was completely charmed, both by the town, and by a young widow, Mrs. Fitzherbert, whom he married in secret some two years later. Needing a home in Brighton, the Prince rented what was called 'a superior farmhouse' in 1787, which he enlarged and developed over the following thirty years to create the Royal Pavilion as it now stands. Over the years the Prince hosted glittering balls, receptions, dinners and parties in the sumptuously decorated rooms.

The first additions to the original farmhouse were made in 1787 by the architect Henry Holland, who built a circular saloon screened by columns, and a further wing to balance the proportions of the house, in the elegant Adam style. The interior was decorated with Chinese artifacts and furnishings in 1802, and the following year Indian-style architecture was used for the building of the magnificent stables (now The Dome Theatre). The Regency architect John Nash echoed and embellished the Indian-style in his great transformation of the Pavilion between 1815–1822.

The interior decorations, furniture and furnishings exude oriental fantasy, together with much refinement and finesse. Some of the pieces are of genuine Chinese origin, but most have been made by English craftsmen, in the Chinese style, with a simulated bamboo-effect in beech and satinwood. The superb cast-iron staircases leading from the main corridor have been painted to look as if they were made from finely carved bamboo, which creates a light, delicate, almost fragile appearance.

The sheer luxury and opulence of the Banqueting Room are quite breathtaking. The massive dining table is laid for a royal feast, with crystal, silver and gold. Eight original standard lamps made of porcelain, ormolu and gilt wood, with lotus flower design shades, stand against the walls which are painted with Chinese scenes. The centre-piece in the domed ceiling is an incredible winged dragon, suspended from huge *trompe d'oeil* jungle leaves, which holds an enormous glittering crystal gasolier (gas-lit chandelier).

The Great Kitchen, which served the Banqueting Room, has copper canopies and palm tree designed columns which echo the oriental theme. The menu displayed there lists some 122 dishes which were cooked for a Royal Banquet, and this, together with the vast range of copper pans, moulds, dishes and all kinds of cooking utensils, gives an insight into the gourmet and sybaritic standards enjoyed by the Prince and his guests. Here 'the Prince once dined with his servants, having first laid a red cloth on the floor.'

The elegant Music Room, where guests were entertained by such illustrious musicians as the composer Rossini, was subjected to a fire-bomb attack in 1975, which caused a great deal of damage. However, the subsequent restoration has revealed the original decorations to be much more beautiful and subtle than was apparent before the fire, due to the extensive overpainting which had taken place over decades.

After the death of King George IV in 1830, his brother and successor, King William IV, faithfully maintained the Pavilion. However, early in the reign of Queen Victoria, the town of Brighton with its many day trippers was deemed to offer too little privacy for royal taste, and the Queen decided to sell the Pavilion to pay for extensions to her new home, Buckingham Palace. In 1850, after much discussion, and many committee meetings, the Brighton Town Councillors purchased the Pavilion for the town, from the Crown Estates for £53,000.

Sadly, all the furniture and furnishings, china and glass, and even murals, wallpapers and decorated doors were removed before the sale, and transported on carrier's carts from Brighton to Buckingham Palace or Windsor Castle. In 1851, the year of the Great Exhibition at Crystal Palace, just one year after buying the empty shell, the new owners held an Opening Ball in the re-decorated Pavilion, and from then on it was used for civic and public functions.

By 1863 Queen Victoria gave permission for some of the furniture and furnishings to be returned, and more were sent back by Queen Mary in the 1920s and 1930s. During the First World War, at the suggestion of King George V, the Pavilion was used as a hospital for Indian soldiers. Since the end of the Second World War interest in the Pavilion has greatly increased, and more recently an intensive restoration programme has been in progress. Wallpaper, carpets and other decorations have been constructed from original fragments and patterns, while materials and methods compatible with those originally used have been employed in the structural restorations.

The Star Inn and Alfriston Village

T HE ancient Star Inn, situated in the centre of Alfriston, one of the prettiest of the East Sussex villages, seems to be the very quintessence of an old English hostelry. Founded in the thirteenth century, the present inn dates from about 1450, and according to local history, was often used as a resting place for pilgrims travelling to the tomb of St. Richard at Chichester (the Sanctuary post can be seen near the door of the Bar inside the inn).

The traditional black and white half-timbered façade is beautifully preserved, and medieval carvings can be seen on some of the timbers. Standing guard, outside at the corner of the inn, there is a ship's figurehead which, according to legend, was brought to Alfriston by smugglers from a Dutch ship wrecked at nearby Cuckmere Haven in the seventeenth century. The old oak door and open fireplaces date from Tudor times, and the roof of the inn is tiled with slabs of Horsham stone, one piece alone weighing some two hundredweight (112 kilos).

The village of Alfriston was built on the site of an old Saxon settlement, and is listed in the Domesday survey. Local archæological excavations have uncovered many Saxon utensils, weapons and coins, as well as Saxon graves.

In 1405, King Henry IV granted the village a charter to hold markets. The Market Cross, which can still be seen, was erected to remind traders that they were bound to deal honestly with their customers.

Alfriston Church, sometimes called 'The Cathedral of the Downs' because of its proportions, has much fine square knapped flint work, and a metal ring on the north-east corner of the tower which held a brazier for signalling invasion. The Easter Sepulchre, one of three left in Sussex, is in the chancel, and the north transept windows have original tracery. There has been a church on this site since 1272, and the present church was built in 1360, as was the nearby Clergy House. Possibly built to house a group of parish priests, the Clergy House was the first building ever to be acquired by the National Trust, in 1869, and it is now open to the public between April and October. Constructed of wattle and daub, the house has the original main frame oak timbers which were ordered and carved for the building. The crownpost roof has a superb thatch, and the floors are made of rammed chalk, sealed with sour milk.

With its large church and market, Alfriston became the centre of the local rural community. Just a few miles from the sea, Alfriston was considered to be a port until 1733, and barges were used to bring goods to the village until 1915.

In the High Street there are houses with names such as *The Old Apiary*, and *Tallow Chandlery*, evoking old industries. There is also a row of cottages which were used for billeting soldiers during the Napoleonic Wars. It is interesting to note that two old Sussex words — *twitten* meaning alleyway, and *tye* for open grass area, are used in the Alfriston village plan.

The Lanes

The atmosphere of old Brighton can be easily experienced by a walk through The Lanes, a maze of inter-connecting alleys and passageways. Originally an area of fishermen's cottages, the old buildings now house antique shops, galleries, small restaurants and pubs. This is the place to find interesting old jewellery of coral, ivory, jade, jet and quartz alongside cameos, old lace and silver photograph frames, in varying quality and state of repair. Collector's items such as old bank notes, coins and sepia postcards, as well as connoisseur's oil paintings, water colours and silver can all be found. The nostalgic theme is underlined by a shop with 'Bespoke Perfumery', and another selling spices, preserves and herbal remedies. There are boutiques with period clothes, modern designer items and pavement racks of current street fashion. Several small restaurants serve traditional fish dishes as well as the French speciality *moules marinière*.

42

Steyning Church

S т. Andrew's Church, Steyning, with its magnificent Romanesque nave, is one of the most interesting churches in Sussex. Rebuilt, and renamed after the fisherman saint, in the twelfth century, St. Andrew's has a fascinating history. The first small wooden church on this site was built in the early ninth century by the Celtic Christian Saint Cuthman, probably on a site of early pagan worship. This overbuilding was the practice of Christian missionaries, in their efforts to prevent any possible reversion to paganism. There are two remaining Saxon stones to be seen in the church porch. One may have been the grave stone of the Saxon King Ethelwulf, father of Alfred the Great (the King 'who burnt the cakes'), who was buried in this church in 858 AD; and the other, with its strange markings, rediscovered in 1938 (after being used as a step for many generations), could well be an original Saxon Standing Stone, which the Saxons set up in early places of worship.

This first church was called St. Cuthman's, and after the death of the founding saint it became a place of pilgrimage, where, it was said, 'marvellous cures were effected for the sick and crippled'. According to legend, St. Cuthman 'left his native Wessex and pulled his crippled mother on a handcart with him, settling to build a church on the spot where the pulling ropes finally gave way' . . . 'at this sequestered place, below the round Hill, where two streams meet'. This story has been dramatized in the play, *Boy with the Cart*, by Christopher Fry. St. Cuthman's became part of a monastery settlement by the end of the ninth century, and was owned by the Saxon kings.

During the eleventh century, the lands and revenues from Steyning Church and Manor were given as a gift to the Norman Abbey of Fecamp by King Edward the Confessor, in return for hospitality he received there whilst in exile. King Harold, Edward's successor, disposed Fecamp of this income, and William Duke of Normandy listed the seizure of Steyning Church as one more reason for the invasion of England. After the Battle of Hastings, Steyning Church was restored to Fecamp, by a charter made in 1085, a copy of which can be seen in the church. By the mid-twelfth century the Norman monks from Fecamp had brought Caen stone across the Channel and built a new church in similar style to the churches in Normandy. The dedication was changed at this time from that of St Cuthman to St. Andrew.

The plan drawing, which can be seen at the west end of the church, shows the original Norman cruciform design. In 1290 the church was described as a Royal Free Chapel, exempt from any ecclesiastical jurisdiction, except that of the Pope. In 1461 the church and its endowments became part of the Briggittine Monastry of Syon in Middlesex, who held them until the suppression of the monastries in 1534.

The church today consists of a chancel, an aisled and clerestoried nave with south porch, and a massive west tower, built around the year 1600, which contains much reused stone and flint building material. The interior of the church was refurbished in 1983, and during this time a chapel in the south aisle of the chancel was dedicated to St. Cuthman, and marked by a new stained glass window. Also at this time, a beautifully carved Tudor oak reredos (ornamental screen), which had formerly been in the old vicarage was placed in position behind the altar on the east wall.

A list of vicars, dating from 1307, together with a series of portraits, and early views of the church, can be seen in the new choir vestry.

Sompting Church with its Saxon tower and helm roof